An Angel's Guide to Enlightenment

B. Empress

BALBOA.
PRESS
A DIVISION OF HAY HOUSE

Balboa Press books may be ordered through booksellers or by contacting:

Balboa Press
A Division of Hay House
1663 Liberty Drive
Bloomington, IN 47403
www.balboapress.com
1-(877) 407-4847

ISBN: 978-1-4525-4745-9 (hc)
ISBN: 978-1-4525-4744-2 (sc)
ISBN: 978-1-4525-4743-5 (e)

Library of Congress Control Number: 2012902635

Printed in the United States of America

Balboa Press rev. date: 4/19/2012

Contents

ACKNOWLEDGEMENTS

Special thanks to Star, who taught me to trust myself. To Angie, who taught me to accept myself. To Raja, who taught me non-separation and Hannon (Whole Spirit), who united me with my Christ-Self.

Introduction

This book is a result of my own journey or path to Enlightenment. The journey stemmed from my need to find a light out of my own personal darkness. I prayed for understanding of God's plan for me. I asked God to help me find a way to release my pain, fears, past childhood traumas and find Enlightenment.

My awareness of god's plan for me was made known through his/her messengers, which are ANGELS. My angel guides explained that I was a Channel for God's Peace. They told me that I was a light and bearer of the book of knowledge.

An Angel's Guide to Enlightenment is dedicated to all who are searching for the light in their own personal darkness. It is written in a step-by-step format, for understanding and achieving Unconditional Love, Happiness, Peace Abundance and Joy.

IT IS A GIFT FORM GOD TO YOU THIS DAY!

GOD BLESS

Part One

CHAPTER 1

ENLIGHTENMENT— HOW DO I GET THERE FROM HERE?

I came to a point in my life, when I decided to turn my life over to God, not to the punishing vengeful God I was brought up to believe in, instead I would turn it over to a God of my creation, which was all loving, all forgiving, and all knowing. I told God that my life was being turned over to him/her: I prayed, put my life on hold and sat waiting for the Burning Bush!

I was out of work, my money was running out, I was nervous and fearful. Two months went by, and no Burning Bush. By chance, I heard about a meditation group that had just started. I had missed one class, and the next class was taking place the next day, in which I could still join. The class was free, so I had nothing to lose. I decided that if God had a message for me, he/she could find me at the class.

That evening I went home, and waited in anticipation of the next day. I was full of emotions; I was excited, happy, and yet fearful because I had been taught that these things are from the devil. I overrode my fears, with the belief that I would know in the first class, if this class were from the light or the darkness.

The next day I went to the class. The teacher was an older woman who explained that the class was made from channeled material. She told us that her classed were blessed with a white light of protection.

I did not understanding what she was talking about, but my gut feeling told me I was safe, and I liked and trusted her.

She spoke to us for a while, and then told us it was time to meditate. She dimmed the lights, put on some weird music, told us to sit comfortably, and close our eyes. She told us to envision a bright white light, to follow that light to a place where our subconscious was, and to ask our subconscious what his/her name was.

I went into the light, and saw a very little old man, with a long white beard and a wizard's outfit. I asked him his name, and he said Tom. He lead me through a tunnel to a mountain, and it was there, he introduced me to some of my angel guides.

I loved the experience, but when I came out of the meditation I became fearful, because I had been told that demons could disguise themselves. My meditation teacher told me that all I had to do was ask them if they were from the light. That they could not lie, and if they were not from the white light, I could tell them to leave.

That night when I went home and meditated, I closed my eyes and asked them if they were from the light, and the answer was yes! From that night on, my loneliness and despair left. I came to understand that we are never really alone.

CHAPTER 2

THE BURNING BUSH— (ANGEL MESSAGES)

Two weeks late, I experienced (Metaphorically speaking), the Burning Bush! It happened while I was having lunch at a fast food restaurant; I heard a voice say, "Write this down!" I looked around to see who said it, but on one was there. I heard the vice again say, "Write this down!" So I took a paper and pen and started to write:

YOU KNOW THY PURPOSE TODAY. YOU ARE A LIGHT OF THE WORLD. YOUR SOUL IS UNITED WITH HIM WHO LOVES YOU. A BLESSING AND GREETINGS TO YOU, BY HIM WHO LOVES YOU.

A CONNECTION IS MADE TODAY, GO IN PEACE AND SPREAD THE GOOD NEWS. GOD IS ETERNAL. GOD IS ALIVE AND WELL AND WITH YOU ALL. THE WHOLE

SPIRIT IS UPON YOU. CONNECTION IS MADE TODAY. GO IN PEACE. LOVE AND CHARITY BE OUR GIFTS.

DO NOT FEEL A HEAVY BURDEN. THE ANSWER OF WHAT TO DO WILL BE REVEALED TO YOU IN GOD'S TIME. TRUST YOUR KNOWLEDGE, AND KNOW THIS IS A GIFT FROM GOD TO YOU THIS DAY.

A DOVE SITS ON YOUR LEFT SHOULDER AND SPEAKS IN YOUR EAR. YOU HAVE KNOCKED AT THE DOOR OF KNOWLEDGE AND HAVE BEEN TOLD TODAY, THE DOOR IS OPEN TO ENTER. PICK UP YOUR CROSS AND FOLLOW ME.

CALL ME HANNON (DOVE OF KNOWLEDGE), THE WHOLE SPIRIT. THE ANSWERS WILL BE KNOWN TO YOU. YOUR SPIRIT HAS TOUCHED THE EAR OF GOD.

When I finished writing, I felt a peace I had never felt before. I knew that this was a message from God, because I had no thought while I was writing. I was writing each word as a separate entity unto itself, and as each word came, I had no conscious thought of what the next word would be, or what the message was.

CHAPTER 3

MORE ANGEL MESSAGES

As weeks passed on, the messages came at what might judge the weirdest times. There was no spiritual pose needed, no chanting was required. I learned that UNIVERSAL TRUTH comes simply when you are open, nothing more is required!

I was sitting watching television when this message came:

LET THERE BE A DAY, WHEN ONE WILL HEAR AND FEEL THE CRY OF ONE WHO IS LOST TO UNIVERSAL TRUTH. AS I SPEAK, OTHERS CRY OUT FOR PEACE, YET HAVE NO CONCEPT OF WHAT IT IS, OR WHEN THEY DO UNDERSTAND, IT IS TO NO AVAIL. MANY WILL RECEIVE THE LIGHT; OTHERS WILL FIND IT AND LOSE IT, WHILE OTHERS WILL USE IT FOR SYNTHESIS. MANY WILL HEAR, YET CLOSE THEMSELVES TO THE TRUTH. OTHERS WILL HEAR,

BUT NOT UNDERSTAND THAT CONQUEST OF (FEAR + EGO) IS NECESSARY FOR TRANSFORMATION! FOR SOME THE PRICE IS TO HIGH TO PAY. YET OTHERS KNOWING THE GIFTS OFFERED, WILL DISCARD THEM LIKE AN OLD SHOE. YOU ARE A MESSENGER OF THE LIGHT NOW. UNION IN THE SPIRIT IS ESSENTIAL, FOR EMOTIONAL GROWTH IS AT HAND.

ALL THAT IS NEEDED IS CHRIST CONSCIOUSNESS AND REBIRTH, WHICH ARE ONE AND THE SAME. RESPONSE TO THE LIGHT IS MOST IMPORTANT, FOR IT IS BENEFICIAL FOR ALL. NOW IS THE TIME FOR YOU TO CONQUER SELF AND FIND SELF-ACTUALIZATION IN THE SPIRIT. I AM GLAD TO BE OF SERVICE TO YOU, AND SHARE THE GIFT OF KNOWLEDGE WITH YOU. ALWAYS KNOW NY INTENT IS PURE. WE ARE ALL ONE IN THE SPIRIT.

GOD BLESS! RAJA.

The concepts of Transformation, Christ Consciousness, and Rebirth sounded great. Yet, I thought to myself "How Do I Get There From Here?"

CHAPTER 4

THE PATH

It was several days later when I received this message:

RELIGION WAS MADE TO TEACH UNITY. IT IS AN
IMPORTANT STEP FOR EACH ENTITY TO LOSE
SELF, AND UNITE WITH EACH SOUL TO LEARN
LOVE. RELIGION WAS CREATED TO TEACH UNITY,
YET A FORM OF SEPARATION HAS OCCURRED. IT
IS NECESSARY TO REUNITE WITH THE FATHER/
MOTHER GOD.

TODAY IS MOST IMPORTANT FOR YOU TO CONTINUE
ON YOUR PATH FOR THE DAY IS COMING, WHEN ALL
WILL HEAR MY CRY FOR PEACE AND LOVE. WHEN
PEACE AND LOVE ARE COMBINED, THEY BRING ALL
GIFTS TO SPIRIT. ABUNDANCE AND PROSPERITY
ARE BUT BY PRODUCTS OF THIS PROCESS.

THE DIRECTION IS MOST IMPORTANT, ONLY THROUGH THE FATHER/MOTHER COMES THE ANSWER. EACH CHILD IS A SEED TO GOD. DIRECTION BE KNOWN TO YOUR TODAY. YOU ARE A LIGHT OF THE WORLD.

DIRECTION IS KNOWN TO YOU TODAY. DEATH OF THE SELF AND REBIRTH ARE ESSENTIAL ELEMENTS IN OUR FATHER/MOTHER PLAN FOR YOU. YOU HAVE A SPIRITUAL PATH TO FOLLOW. MANY HEALING GIFTS ARE AVAILABLE TO YOU WHEN YOUR PROCESS IS COMPLETE

A SEVEN-MONTH WAITING PERIOD IS REQUIRED. IF YOU STAY ON THE PATH THE END IS NEAR, SO THE BEGINNING CAN START. FULL CIRCLE IS NEEDED, FOR YOUR SPIRIT WILL REJOIN IN THE THIRD OF DECEMBER. DO NOT BE BURDENED OR FEARFUL. ALL IS POSSIBLE. THE PATH IS AS EASY, AS A CHILD IS PROTECTED AND GUIDED WITH HER PARENT AT BIRTH, SO WILL YOU BE, TIME IS NOT IMPORTANT TO YOU ANYMORE.

THE FATHER/MOTHER KNOWS YOUR HOUR IS COMING, BE HUMBLE, GRATEFUL, AND NOT AFRAID. YOUR PATH IS AS BEAUTIFUL AS A SUNSET, AND AS PEACEFUL AS A DOVE. LOVE AND PEACE BE WITH YOU ALWAYS. THE TIME IS COMING, REJOICE!

After I read the message a question, came to me. How do I stay on the path? The answer came to me:

YOU NEED ONLY BE OPEN TO THE TRUTH AND THE VOICE OF GOD.

I found daily prayer and meditation were the keys to keep my path will lighted.

CHAPTER 5

THE ROCK ON THE PATH

I enjoyed receiving the messages, and my life was peaceful. My mind questioned, when was this transformation going to take place? I wondered what I would be like after. What miracles I would be a part of.

In the past, I had always waited for my angel guides to contact me. I decided to try to call them and ask them some questions. I thought I might seem like a nut, but I had nothing to lose. I called them and this was the message I received:

AS THE EYE OF THE TORNADO DEVELOPS ALL IS CALM. ENJOY THE LAST DAYS, BEFORE YOU ARE CALLED TO DO BATTLE WITH THE EGO.

I did not really understand the message, so I asked for clarification. The message was as follows:

YOU CAN STAY ON THE PATH OF ENLIGHTENMENT AND GO THROUGH THE ROCK, IT WILL TAKE SIX MONTHS, OR YOU CAN TAKE TWENTY YEARS. THE CHOICE IS YOURS!

TO GO THROUGH THE ROCK, YOU MUST HAVE FAITH THAT YOU WILL BE ABLE TO COME OUT ON THE OTHER SIDE. EVEN IN THE DARKNESS THE LIGHT WILL SHINE IF YOU HAVE FAITH. ENJOY YOUR PEACE. YOUR TIME IS COMING. THE CHOICE IS YOURS. RAJA.

I wanted enlightenment yesterday. So I thought, why not get it over in six months, rather than wait twenty years. I chose the six months. Although, an old saying, my mom use to say came to mind, which was: "Be careful what you ask for, you just might get it."

CHAPTER 6

THE BOOK

The peace I was feeling began to lessen, because of my apprehension of what was to come. I did not know that was going to happen on a conscious level although, I was sure my subconscious knew.

I kept busy, and had daily prayer and meditation. I found that for the first time, I had no conscious memory of my meditations. I was to find out later, that not remembering had been my choice, nothing mysterious about it. I guess I chose this, to avoid becoming fearful of what was ahead for me.

I called Hannon, and asked: Why will these experiences be happening to me? The answer was:

IN YOU JOURNEY STAY ON THE PATH, EVEN IF OTHERS DO NOT UNDERSTAND US. A HEALING IS AT HAND. REMEMBER GOD HAS CHOSEN YOU

TO RECEIVE HIS/HER GIFTS OF ABUNDANCE AND PEACE. REMEMBER YOUR ARE OUR LIGHT AND BEARER OF THE BOOK OF KNOWLEDGE. PLEASE STAY GROUNDED.

NOW SPREAD THE GOOD NEWS, THAT ALL MAY RECEIVE THESE GIFTS. KNOCK AND THE DOOR WILL BE ANSWERED. LOVE, PEACE AND JOY ARE YOUR GIFTS TODAY. PEACE IS WITH YOU. HANNON (DOVE OF KNOWLEDGE.) PRAISE GOD!

I sat on the couch thinking, am I going to write a book? I do not even like to write a letter. I make long distance calls to avoid writing. As I looked at the message, a memory came to surface. I remembered as a child telling my mom, that I was going to write a book some day. I did not know what the book would be about, yet I was sure I would write one. I remember my mom saying, "You can do anything you want to do."

My feelings were that of both, joy and fear. I sat thinking that this may be the reason I came here, this maybe my purpose, the reason for my existence on this planet. Having been taught that when you do what you came to do you die, I became fearful to that which I wanted to be most, a CHANNEL FOR GOD'S PEACE. I learned to overcome this fear, as time went on. I came to understand that we are masters of our own fate. That good does not have to precede bad! The good and bad do not exist. The choice to die is ours. The choice to live is ours. The choice to be happy is ours. The choice to be sad is ours, IN SPITE OF APPEARANCES!

CHAPTER 7

GOING THROUGH THE ROCK

I came to understand that to become a clear channel one must let go of self-deception. The battle of the ego my angel guides spoke about, had to do with acceptance of myself, self-forgiveness for my trespasses and forgiveness of others for their actions. I had blocked and built walls to hide from myself, my experiences as they were. I painted a picture of what I wish to remember, and buried all unpleasant experiences I wished to forget. I found that these experiences were the foundation of my karma. I found that hiding from the truth was impossible.

Let's say that every time we created dirty clothes, we put them in a closet and denied their existence. Year after year, we put our dirty laundry in our own private closet. Eventually, we are unable to close the closet. We now may face it, or we may need something to help us forget. For some, this is a drug. For others it may be liquor, for some food, for others it may be worrying about things that might happen, for others it may manifest in the form of violence, ECT.

If we wish to avoid looking at ourselves in the light of truth, we may have chosen these forms of distraction, as a means to avoid looking at our dirty laundry or garbage. Unfortunately it does not end here, because running away from ourselves is impossible.

This process of self-condemnation creates new karma. Which in turn we need to put in our closet. As our house becomes over crowed with all this dirty laundry or garbage, we come to feel isolated and alone. We may choose to experience illness as an escape. This is another form of distraction. Illness is only a reflection on the outside, of our internal struggle to rid ourselves of that loneliness, and to ultimately bring us into the light again. Illness is one way, in which an entity may choose to come to self-acceptance. The choice is always yours.

A more direct way of coming to the light is going through the rock, which is the fastest. Going through the rock, is taking a step with God at your side, into your own personal traumas, hates, resentments, and fears, in order to be born again. Being born again means washing away our sins, which comes from self-forgiveness, and self-acceptance, which includes forgiveness of all and acceptance of all, in order to learn the lesson. Acceptance of all does not imply being a doormat. Simply put, it is self-acceptance because we are one in the spirit. The choice to live in denial is to remain in separation, which means we keep repeating the same experiences, in order to learn the lesson.

We may find we have the same experiences with the people; the only difference is the name and the face. We have put ourselves in a maze, going around and around, without knowing the way out.

The solution is simple. Ask your God to help you out. Be open to face yourself in the light of truth. Our self-created bogeymen are our own fears, hates and resentments. Having the faith to face our past, our pain, and our fears in the light of truth, enables us to be free! In the light of truth, we are made whole and are born again.

Having survived the experience, I can assure you, it was worth the feeling and emotions I experienced. I had run away from these feeling my whole life. Yet facing these emotions and accepting all of my life experiences enabled me to find a peace and understanding that could not have been internalized without my own personal experience.

The next chapters are dedicated to all who are searching for the light in their own personal darkness. It is a seep by step process for understanding and achieving unconditional love, happiness, peace, abundance, and joy!

IT IS A GIFT FROM GOD TO YOU THIS DAY!

God Bless

Part Two

TERMINOLOGY

ANGEL—Let's speak of TRUTH.

ANGER—Let's speak of JUSTIFICATION.

BETRAYAL—Let's speak of EXPECTATIONS.

DEATH—Let's speak of TRANSFORMATION.

DENIAL—Let's speak of SEPARATION
(feelings of isolation and emptiness).

FEAR—Let's speak of PROJECTION.

FEELINGS OF LACK—Let's speak of DENIAL.

FORGIVENESS—Let's speak of SELF-FORGIVENESS.

GOOD AND BAD—Let's speak of JUDGMENT.

GUILT—Let's speak of SELF-PUNISHMENT.

HAPPINESS—Let's speak of TRUTH (ONENESS).

HATE—Let's speak of FEAR.

HOPE—Let's speak of CONNECTION (ONENESS).

INSANITY—Let's speak of SEPARATION INTENSIFIED.

JEALOUSY—Let's speak of DENIAL.

JUDGMENT—Let's speak of DENIAL/SEPARATION.

LIFE—Let's speak of PERCEPTION.

LONELINESS—Let's speak of SELF-CONDEMNATION (DENIAL).

LOVE—Let's speak of SELF-LOVE.

OPINION Let's speak of JUDGMENT.

REJECTION—Let's speak of SEPARATION.

TRUTH—Let's speak of ONENESS.

CHAPTER EIGHT

THE NINE STAGES OF CREATION

(LEVELS TWO PHYSICAL/MENTAL)

9. **VOID (GOD CONSCIOUSNESS):** PRE-THOUGHT, BEFORE CREATION, PURE ESSENCE, AND PURE LOVE. (EMBRACEMENT OF ALL.)

8. **THOUGHT (CREATING):** ELECTRONS, NEUTRONS, PROTONS, JOIN TOGETHER IN AGREEMENT TO FORM AN ATOM.

7. **CREATING:** COLOR, CREATING MASS WITH DISTINCTIVE PROPERTIES, GIVING SUBSTANCE AND MASS. CREATING PROPERTIES WITHIN THAT SUBSTANCE SUCH AS, SOLIDS LIQUIDS, AND GAS.

6. **CREATING SOUND:** VIBRATION IS CREATED IN THIS LEVEL.

5. **ELECTROLYTES:** LIGHT SPINNING, PROPERTIES OF ELECTROLYTES. LIGHT IS SPINNING GAINING MOMENTUM. IN THIS STAGE EVERYTHING IS IN CONSTANT MOTION.

4. **ANIMATION:** IMAGINATION.

3. **VACUUM:** BRINGING THOUGHTS INTO MANIFESTATION.

2. **LIGHT STAGE:** IMAGE MORE SOLID.

ASTRAL: **THERE ARE THREE STAGES**:

(THIRD ASTRAL)—FORM NOT COMPLETELY SOLID.

(SECOND ASTRAL)—CONSISTS OF MINERAL AND ROCKS.

(FIRST ASTRAL)—ASTRAL INCARNATE FORM LAST PHYSICAL.

THE TRINITY

MIND—FATHER
PHYSICAL—TRANSMUTATION
SPIRIT—WHOLE SPIRIT

MIND—(VOID CONSCIOUSNESS). Is the (FATHER) CHRIST spoke of.

PHYSICAL—(BODY) is the (SON). TRANSMUTATION, which is the VIBRATORY CHANGE RATE into the physical.

SPIRIT—(WHOLE SPIRIT). Is the (COLLECTIVE CONSCIOUSNESS) Of ALL

ATOM AND EVE

The TEMPTATION the bible speaks about is JUDGMENT (SEPARATION AND DENIAL). SELF-IMPOSED LIMITATIONS—Which brought SIN. (SIN IS DISCONNECTION WITH GOD!) It is caused by our denial of oneness.

IT IS OUR DENIAL OF ONENESS

> Which brought about REJECTION—
>> Which is SEPARATION.
> Which brought about FEAR—
>> Which is PROJECTION.
> Which brought about ANGER—
>> Which is JUSTIFICATION.
> Which brought about feeling of LACK—
>> Which is DENIAL.
> Which brought about GUILT—
>> Which is SELF-PUNISHMENT.
> Which brought about LONELINESS—
>> Which is SELF-CONDEMNATION.
> Which brought about FORGIVENESS—
>> Which is SELF-FORGIVENESS.

Which brought about LOVE—
> Which is SELF-LOVE.

Which brought about DEATH—
> Which is TRANSFORMATION.

Which brought about TRUTH—
> Which is ONENESS.

Which brought about HAPPINESS.

LETS SPEAK ABOUT TRUTH!

FAITH = BELIEF
WITHOUT DOUBT

The temptation CHRIST spoke about is the (BIG I), SEPARATION, which is JUDGMENT.

Lead us not into temptation equals—OLD PATTERNS and OLD TAPES.

Satan—is men and women in SEPARATION/JUDGMENT, (OLD TAPES AND OLD PATTERNS).

Faith equals—Belief that you can overcome the temptation (JUDGMENT). That in essence GOD is more powerful than Satan. Ask and it shall be given. The universe is at your beckon call. You are whole and not alone. Everything you need to know, or understand is given instantly as long as you have FAITH (NO DOUBT), that it will be given.

BELIEF SYSTEM

AS I PERCEIVE I RECEIVE. As I perceive life, (LIFE IS).
I create my existence in a three-fold way—MIND
BODY AND SOUL

MIND (THOUGHT)
BODY (VOICED)
SOUL (BELIEF)
IN AGREEMENT

This is how it is done. First was the thought, than the
spoken word (AFFIRMATION), and finally, the belief of
the TRUTH. Agreement has been made (Three Fold Way);
therefore manifestation is now in process. Your Belief System,
consisting of Thought, Affirmation (Spoken Word), and Belief
(AGREEMENT), which CREATES YOUR LIFE!

AS YOU PERCEIVE YOU RECEIVE.

QUESTIONS AND ANSWERS

STUDENT: How do I stop my fears from becoming a MANIFESTATION?

ANGEL: Simple, use this the three fold process.

THE THREE-FOLD PROCESS

STEP 1. Ask yourself to be aware when you voice "negative statements".

STEP 2. When you hear yourself saying a negative statement, VOID IT!

STEP 3. The BELIEF of the NEW STATEMENT brings into MANIFESTATION the new reality.

EXAMPLE—Let's say you are with your co-workers or friends and they start to say something "negative", and you start to agree with them, STOP and say NO, I TAKE IT BACK! Voice what you wish to make your NEW REALITY. This may seem foolish to some. Know that when we go against UNIVERSAL TRUTH WE DENY OUR TRUE SELF. UNIVERSAL TRUTH is the key to all that makes us happy.

STUDENT—I would feel embarrassed to say it out loud could I just think it?

ANGEL—   It would be best once a thought is voiced, to
VOID it with another STATEMENT, to give
it the same power as the last one. The BELIEF
Of the voiced NEW STATEMENT, brings into
MANIFESTATION the NEW REALITY.

REMEMBER, AS YOU PERCEIVE YOU RECEIVE!

ONENESS

FAITH is the evidence of ONENESS IN SPITE OF THE APPEARANCE.

The BODY is the process of voiced affirmation (I AM). Through this process GOD became all that is of the physical form, and all that is not of the physical form. The putting into action (I AM), of the physical, offered a new way of life gained by the realization of "who" (I AM).

We first have THE THOUGHT (I AM). Now with the understanding of oneness, we can begin the process of changing our LIFE, through our thoughts and voiced affirmations.

THE KEY TO A BETTER SELF-IMAGE
IS NON-JUDGMENT.

(FORGIVENESS IS THE FIRST STEP
TO NON-JUDGMENT).

THE TRINITY

GOD

333

THREE LEVELS

MIND BODY SOUL

(FATHER) (SON) (WHOLE SPIRIT)

SATAN

SATAN

666

A Six is a Three Reversed and Closed off. Which equals Denial of the Body, Mind, and Soul.

SATAN = SEPARATION FORM GOD

SATAN RULES EARTH = MEN AND WOMEN WITHOUT GOD CONSCIOUSNESS

GOD CONSCIOUSNESS EQUALS = PURE ESSENCE AND UNCONDITIONAL LOVE

SATAN = THE BIG (I)

THE BIG I = JUDGMENT I SEPARATE

(WHEN I JUDGE I SEPARATE MYSELF)

THE BIG (I) IS ALSO TERMED EGO.

EGO = NOTHING TO FEAR, BECAUSE
IT IS NON-EXISTENT.

CHAPTER NINE

JUDGMENT (I) SEPARATE

WHEN I JUDGE (I) SEPARATE, WHICH IS DENIAL.
THE BIG (I) IS TERMED THE EGO

The EGO is nothing to fear, because it does not exist. The EGO is the illusion of separation. The EGO was a term we created, in an attempt to reunite ourselves, and feel whole. The EGO, attempts to repair itself into becoming whole again, through experience, understanding, and growth in order to reunite, and renew itself with the one source, which is UNIVERSAL CONSCIOUSNESS (ONENESS).

JUDGMENT = DENIAL = SEPARATION

WHICH IN TURN = ILLUSION OF THE EGO THE BIG (I)

EXPERIENCE + GROWTH + RENEWED
UNDERSTANDING = UNIVERSAL

CONSCIOUSNESS, WHICH IS (GOD CONSCIOUSNESS)

The EGO is not our enemy; it is a part of the GOD CONSCIOUSNESS, trying to bring us back to universal consciousness and wholeness. When we stop judging our actions, and the actions of other, SEPARATION IS NO MORE AND WE ARE HOME AGAIN IN UNIVERSAL CONSCIOUSNESS.

LIGHT—LIFE—JOY—LOVE

(THE BIG I)

JUDGMENT (I) SEPARATE

I AM BETTER THEN YOU.

I AM LESS THEN YOU.

VS

I AM YOU, AND WE ARE ONE.

When we realize we are all one, and let go of the big (I), then

JUDGMENT AND SEPARATION ARE GONE.

CHAPTER TEN

KEYS TO LIFE

What is the key to peace?—UNCONDITIONAL LOVE.

What is the key to abundance?—UNCONDITIONAL LOVE.

What is the key to happiness?—UNCONDITIONAL LOVE.

What is the key to poverty?—UNCONDITIONAL LOVE.

What is the key to remove loneliness?—UNCONDITIONAL LOVE.

What is the key to restore health?—UNCONDITIONAL LOVE.

CHAPTER ELEVEN

NINE STEPS TO FEEL UNCONDITIONAL LOVE

STEP 1. Faith (belief without doubt).

STEP 2. Self-forgiveness.

STEP 3. Forgiveness of others.

STEP 4. Self-acceptance.

STEP 5. Acceptance of others.

STEP 6. Let go of Judgment/Separation.

STEP 7. Give to yourself first.

STEP 8. Give to others as you give to yourself.

STEP 9. Practice the laws of abundance.

REMEMBER—SELF-ACCEPTANCE + SELF-FORGIVENESS = SELF-LOVE, WHICH IN RETURN GIVES US UNCONDITIONAL LOVE FOR ALL.

CHAPTER TWELVE

HOW TO DEVELOP FAITH

STEP 1.   Know that I am a child of GOD.

STEP 2.   Know that GOD flows through me continuously, in spite of appearances.

STEP 3.   Know that FAITH is my awareness of that continuous flow.

STEP 4.   Feel the FLOW.

STEP 5.   Share your knowledge of faith with others (AFFIRMATIONS).

STEP 6.   Practice FAITH continuously.

STEP 7.   Know that everything you ask for, is already being MANIFESTED, and only awaits your permission to come into your awareness.

CHAPTER THIRTEEN

THE TRINITY

THE NUMBER OF GOD IS 333

THE TRINITY IS 3 TIMES 3

TOTAL 9 STAGES

PHYSICAL (BODY) HAS THREE STAGES

MENTAL (GOD CONSCIOUSNESS)
HAS THREE STAGES

SPIRIT (WHOLE SPIRIT)

PHYSICAL = PHYSICAL, MENTAL AND SPIRIT.

MENTAL = PHYSICAL, MENTAL AND SPIRIT.

SPIRIT = PHYSICAL, MENTAL AND SPIRIT.

THE PHYSICAL
THREE STAGES

(PHYSICAL PHYSICAL, PHYSICAL MIND
AND PHYSICAL SPIRIT)

PHYSICAL (PHYSICAL) STAGE

PHYSICAL (PHYSICAL)—To bring into direct manifestation, through thought we CREATE and become in ESSENCE the CREATION. No separation in the thought. We become an EXTENSION of that thought. Be at ONE with the THOUGHT and CREATION. Feel your THOUGHTS come into form, going through the LEVELS of MANIFESTED CREATION, through the awareness of yourself in (ONENESS).

PHYSICAL (MIND) STAGE

PHYSICAL (MIND)—Needs to see EROS, which is god in its pure form. Thought is free flowing particles, which consists of electrons, neutrons, and protons. Thought is creation.

EXAMPLE—The student wants to win money. The thought is to win the money. The thought attracts free flowing particles (INCEPTION), and starts to attract (CREATE), an electro-magnetical field him/her, to bring this thought into manifestation. Then denial may come into his/her mind that they probably will not win. That new thought moves EROS away from this field to create the new thought pattern. It is our own thought patterns that create our life.

PHYSICAL (SPIRIT) STAGE

PHYSICAL (SPIRIT)—The whole spirit in agreement (GOD CONSCIOUSNESS). As I say it—it is. No time element. The whole spirit termed the Holy Spirit, which is the single eye no separation.

MENTAL THREE STAGES

(MENTAL PHYSICAL—(CONSCIOUS), IS THE SON)
(MENTAL MIND—(SUBCONSCIOUS),
IS THE FATHER)
(MENTAL SPIRIT—(SUPER-CONSCIOUS),
IS THE WHOLE SPIRIT)

MENTAL (PHYSICAL)—The body is three directional. The mental physical stage is what psychologists have termed the conscious. The mental physical stage is merely an optical illusion of the three dimensional reality, which we call the physical. Our mental physical reality has come into existence though our own thought patterns, which we call the physical. The mental physical (CONSCIOUS), believes the physical to be real, or solid even though they are just a thought projection. They are merely imagination, which has been manifested into this three dimensional physical reality we created. We term this reality our mental physical (CONSCIOUS).

MENTAL (MIND)—Psychologists term the mental mind the subconscious, which is the strainer. It filters information from the super-conscious. The subconscious mind, then takes that which it can assimilate and rejects the rest. Our subconscious mind has the ability through synthesis, to manifest our belief and thoughts into the physical.

MENTAL (SPIRIT)—Psychologists have termed the mental spirit as the super-conscious. The super-conscious is the VOID consciousness, or GOD conscious. Within the super-conscious are the AKASHIC RECORDS. GOD consciousness = no pre-thought, all feeling, pure essence.

Void consciousness is to feel one the father, perceive no separation and to encompass all. In Void consciousness there is nothing to see and nothing to fear, which brings into direct focus of the trinity. This has been termed the CHRIST consciousness.

SPIRIT THREE STAGES

(SPIRIT PHYSICAL—TRANSMUTATION)
(SPIRIT MENTAL—AKASHIC RECORDS)
(SPIRIT SPIRIT—WHOLE SPIRIT)

The SPIRIT (PHYSICAL)—Is the ability to change form. Vibratory rate increases to astral level. Transmutation is the ability to transcend form from one plane to another, no time element.

SPIRIT (MENTAL)—The AKASHIC RECORDS, are at your disposal without the aid of angel guides (NO SEPARATION). The AKASHIC RECORDS contain all information recorded in the universe, such as LEVITATION and MANIFESTATION. DESTINY is the limitation of your evolution. Meaning as you evolve DESTINY ceases to exist.

SPIRIT (SPIRIT)—The WHOLE SPIRIT is the collective consciousness of all. No language barrier. TRANSMUTATION in its purest form means ability to communicate with all because I am ONE with all and has the ability to receive all information in an instant. VOID consciousness has the ability to split levels also in the physical.

CHAPTER FOURTEEN

LET'S SPEAK OF SELF-DECEPTION

1. Feelings of unworthiness.
2. Feeling of lack.
3. Feelings of jealousy.
4. Feeling of loneliness.
5. Feelings of low self-esteem.
6. Feelings of abandonment.
7. Feelings of loss.
8. Feeling of guilt.
9. Feelings of betrayal.

IN ESSENCE WHEN WE SPEAK OF THESE EMOTIONS WE SPEAK OF THE (BIG I).

CHAPTER FIFTEEN

JUDGMENT (I) SEPARATION

(JUDGMENT CAUSES SEPARATION WHICH IS DENIAL)

Remember your wholeness, and remember there is no (I/Separation). It is self-created by perception, through thought, voiced AFFIRMATION and BELIEF. When this happens, you become like a live wire without direction. The solution is simple; just reunite with the source of the flow by:

STEP 1.   Think that you want a conscious contact with your GOD.

STEP 2.   Voice it out loud (AFFIRMATION).

STEP 3.   Believe you will have a conscious contact with your GOD.

ASK AND IT SHALL BE GIVEN.
IMPORTANT—BELIEVE WITHOUT DOUBT!

CHAPTER SIXTEEN

KARMA

(THOUGHTS = MANIFESTATION)
(FEAR = MANIFESTATION)
(SELF-LOVE + SELF-FORGIVENESS = ZERO KARMA)

1. Karma is the evidence of things unseen. Unconditional love. TRANSCENDS karma. SEPARATION/JUDGMENT CREATES KARMA. Karma is a self-imposed limitation. The SELF (EGO) is the thought that creates separation.

2. Universal truth is "I create my own reality or life". My life is a reflection of my thoughts and fears. Karma is a direct result of my thoughts and fears. The key to Karma is SELF-CONDEMNATION. My thoughts create my actions. Without thought there is no action. My thoughts, fears and self-condemnation create my karma.

3. Karma is payment for actions. The payment, or Karma is a direct result of the INDIVIDUAL THINKING PROCESS, which is the individual's OWN JUDGMENT! Judgment is separation. In

order to TRANSCEND Karma, UNCONDITIONAL LOVE is the KEY. Through love and understanding (ONENESS), an entity TRANSCENDS Karma.

4. When we see GOD in all and LOVE UNCONDITIONALLY, without SEPARATION (JUDGMENT), we are free from the bondage or limitation of Karma!

5. KARMA EQUALS: As I give I receive in judgment of separation. In UNIVERSAL CONSCIOUSNESS we transcend Kara judgment of separation, because we know that AS I GIVE, I RECEIVE INSTANTLY AT THE MOMENT OF GIVING BECAUSE I NO LONGER PERCEIVE A SEPARATION.

CHAPTER SEVENTEEN

CHOICES

PRINCIPLES OF ABUNDANCE   VS   PRINCIPLES OF LACK

1. SELF-ACCEPTANCE	1. SELF-CONDEMNATION
2. SELF-FORGIVENESS	2. JUDGMENT/SEPARATION
3. SELF-LOVE	3. KARMA
4. ABUNDANCE	4. FEELING OF LACK

JUDGMENT /SEPARATION—The result is SELF-CONDEMNATION.

SELF-CONDEMNATION—The result is KARMA.

KARMA—the result is the FEELINGS OF LACK.

SELF-FORGIVENESS—The result is SELF LOVE.

SELF-LOVE—The result is ABUNDANCE.

THE MANIFESTATIONS OF THE PHYSICAL ARE A DIRECT RESULT OF WHAT IS HAPPENING INTERNALLY.

CHAPTER EIGHTEEN

~·XXX·~

MANIFESTATION PROCESS WITH SPIRIT

(PRACTICE THE LAWS OF ABUNDANCE)

STEP 1.   (A)   SELF-LOVE.

            (B)   LOVE OTHERS (remember that they are extensions of yourself).

STEP 2.   (A)   GIVE FREELY TO YOURSELF.

            (B)   GIVE FREELY TO OTHERS (remember that they are extensions of yourself).

(SELF-LOVE + LOVE OTHERS) + (GIVE FREELY TO YOURSELF + GIVE FREELY TO OTHERS) = MANIFESTATION OF ABUNDANCE.

REMEMBER "PRACTICE MAKES PERFECT", THE MORE YOU PRACTICE THE PRINCIPLES OF

ABUNDANCE, THE MORE ABUNDANCE WILL FLOW
TO YOU.

WHEN WE PRACTICE THE LAWS OF ABUNDANCE
THE RESULT IS MANIFESTATION OF ABUNDANCE

QUESTIONS TO ANGEL GUIDE

STUDENT: I have seen people who cheat and steal who have abundance without following the steps you have taught me why is that?

ANGEL: Listen to the words, "FEELINGS OF LACK". Many people have a lot of money and "success". Some of these same "successful" people kill themselves, or turn to drugs, as an aid to help themselves live with themselves. The reason is they have FEELINGS OF LACK! They feel empty and alone.

IN ORDER TO TRULY HAVE ABUNDANCE, YOU MUST FOLLOW THESE SIMPLE STEPS IN THEIR PROPER ORDER.

HALF MEASURES BRING INTERESTING RESULTS!

LET'S SPEAK OF GIVING AND RECEIVING

If I shut the door so that you cannot take from me, I also shut the door on receiving. It is a revolving door. Shut the door on giving and you shut the door on receiving because it is the same door for both. It I shut out my brother, I truly shut out myself.

Don't be afraid to open your door. No one can take anything from you, unless you agree to give it to them. Even if you feel you have been taken advantage of in the past. It we look at the situation a little closer, we realize that we were in agreement, because we gave our power to them. We may now regret doing so, but remember, regret is Judgment/Separation. Forgive yourself, and realize that you did the very best you could at the time.

Your actions are always right and perfect. When we think they are not, realize that this thought is your own creation of self-condemnation. Remember that self-condemnation is the first step in creating feelings of lack. Forgive your self, because SELF-ACCEPTANCE is the first step to ABUNDANCE.

REMEMBER YOU HAVE FREE WILL.

THE CHOICE IS YOURS!

CHAPTER NINETEEN

SELF-IMAGE

Your SELF-IMAGE changes, when you let go of both the JUDGMENT of YOURSELF and the JUDGMENT of OTHERS

STEPS TO CHANGE SELF-IMAGE.

1. SELF-LOVE—Understanding that we are all one with the father, so to LOVE YOURSELF truly LOVE EVERYONE, by acknowledging your ONENESS with them.

This is truly SELF-LOVE.

2. SELF-TRUST—This is the process that acknowledges the truth, that we are one and as we forgive others for their actions we truly forgive ourselves.

3. FAITH—The presence of TRUTH in spite of the illusion of
   SEPARATION (APPEARANCE).

SELF-LOVE + SELF-TRUST + FAITH = SELF-ACCEPTANCE
+ ACCEPTANCE OF OTHERS.

CHAPTER TWENTY

VIBRATION RATES

6.5   GATHERING KNOWLEDGE.

7.0   KNOWLEDGE ALREADY IN CONSCIOUSNESS.

8.0   TRANSMISSION OF KNOWLEDGE
      (COMMUNICATION). APPLICATION OF
      KNOWLEDGE.

9.0   KNOWLEDGE RECEIVES THROUGH
      COMMUNICATION. RESULTS OF APPLICATION
      OF KNOWLEDGE.

NOTE:

7.0—IS THE UNIVERSAL NUMBER

8.0—IS THE TRANSMUTATION NUMBER

9.0—IS THE TRANSFORMATION NUMBER

CHAPTER TWENTY-ONE

———≈———

OUR SUBCONSCIOUS

STUDENT: What is Pre-Thought?

ANGEL: Psychologist's term it the subconscious. Our subconscious does our biding, bringing into manifestation on the physical, so that we may understand (learn).

STUDENT: Can you explain how SUBLIMINAL TAPES work?

ANGEL: Subliminal tapes enter into our subconscious (PRE-THOUGHT), and help bring about manifestation into the physical. Conflicting PRE-THOUGHTS bring into manifestation necessary results.

EXAMPLE: A subliminal tape used to give messages of attracting money, goes into our PRE-THOUGHT. Now a student who believes money is the root of (all evil) or feels (low self-esteem) plays the attracting money tape. This enters into the PRE-THOUGHT along with the belief of money is the root of all evil and feeling of low self-esteem. The result is, the student now attracts MONEY PROBLEMS.

This is a result on one's own BELIEF SYSTEM (SPIRITUAL DENIAL). Low self-esteem is a result of denial of your true self. You are a child of GOD. You are ONE with GOD.

STUDENT: How do I CHANGE this result?

(MONEY PROBLEMS)

ANGEL: PRACTICE THE LAWS OF ABUNDANCE FIRST. (SELF-LOVE + LOVE OTHERS) + (GIVE FREELY TO YOURSELF + GIVE FREELY TO OTHERS) = MANIFESTATION OF ABUNDANCE.

Remember, "Practice makes perfect". The more you practice the principles of abundance the more ABUNDANCE will flow to you.

THE UNIVERSAL LESSON TAUGHT HERE IS, AS YOU PERCEIVE YOU RECEIVE! PRE-THOUGHT + THOUGHT + VOICED THOUGHTS = YOUR BELIEF SYSTEM.

YOUR BELIEF SYSTEM EQUALS YOUR LIFE

EXAMPLE: There are some students who say life is hell.

HELL = PRE-THOUGHT + VOICED AFFIRMATION = YOUR LIFE.

ANGEL: Subliminal tapes were made to help us override our "negative" thinking. They are strong images, and enter into our PRE-THOUGHT (SUBCONSCIOUS). PRE-THOUGHT is the physical part of the TRINITY (ONE), the SECOND PLANE OF UNDERSTANDING. Which aids us in directed MANIFESTATION. CONFLICTING PRE-THOUGHTS BRING INTO MANIFESTATION NECESSARY RESULTS!

EXAMPLE: Non-Smoking subliminal tapes are designed to help you override your desire to smoke. A student plays the tape and it tells him/her that he/she does not like to smoke, because it is BAD for his/her health. He/She plays the tape, and it said it is a dirty and dangerous habit. The student already has a PRE-THOUGHT in his/her belief such as a cigarette makes me feel calm. He/She also feels a sense of low self-esteem. This all gets into his/her PRE-THOUGHT (Subconscious). Thoughts MAY come out like this: I don't like to smoke. I think it is a dirty habit. I believe smoking is bad for my health. I need to smoke, because it keeps me calm. THE RESULT MAY BE HEALTH PROBLEMS!

USING PRE-THOUGHT BEFORE THOUGHT IS OUT
OF SEQUENCE USING PRE-THOUGHT ON THE
PHYSICAL IS STEP TWO OF THE TRINITY.

USING SUBLIMINAL TAPES OUT OF SEQUENCE
(BEFORE THOUGHT), WITHOUT UNDERSTANDING
OF THE MENTAL PROCESS, BRINGS ABOUT
NECESSARY RESULTS FOR LEARNING

DRUGS

The Subconscious is the filter, which brings information from the Super Conscious in amounts, which are easily assimilated by the body or conscious. It protects the body or physical from to large a dose of information, which could bring the body or conscious into an unbalanced state. Without the subconscious filter, an entity would be aware of two levels, or plans of reality. This filter or veil is a balancer between the two levels of reality.

DRUGS may open this veil or gate. They bring an alternate state of consciousness or reality. In some cases this experience may cause a state of consciousness call INSANITY. INSANITY is knowledge without understanding. Which may bring a greater degree of imbalance.

TRUTH WITHOUT UNDERSTANDS LEADS TO MANIFESTED FEARS WHICH LEADS TO (DEATH), MEANING NOT OF THIS PLANE AND NOT OF THAT PLANE. A PERSON TERMED A SCHIZOPHRENIC IS AN ENTITY THAT IS IN THIS STATE OF CONSCIOUSNESS. IT IS SOMEONE WHO IS STUCK BETWEEN TWO REALITIES. REMEMBER EVEN THESE EXPERIENCES ARE OF KARMIC CHOICE.

OUR SUBCONSCIOUS

The subconscious is your guide and not a destructive force keeping you from the truth. It is as a mother that teaches and nourishes you until your conscious has expanded to the point when your subconscious no longer must protect you from void consciousness, which is a state of conscious non-separation which we term CHRIST-CONSCIOUSNESS.

STUDENT: What is HYPNOSIS?

ANGEL: Hypnosis is self-induced pre-thought, from subconscious into conscious. Our pre-thought creates a magnetic field, which attracts various experiences and brings them into manifestation for learning.

Experience enables the conscious to redirect thought and the belief system in order to change the magnetic field. When this occurs your LIFE PATTERNS CHANGE.

NO ONE CAN HYPNOTIZE YOU WITHOUT YOUR CONSENT! ALL HYPNOSIS IS SELF-INDUCED!

It is best to know the person you allow to hypnotize you, because this puts you in DIRECTED PRE-THOUGHT suggestions, which create a more direct magnetic field. HYPNOSIS enables you a faster flow of directed manifestation.

CONFLICTING VIEWS OF HYPNOTIC SUGGESTION CAUSES INTERESTING RESULTS!

EXAMPLE: Hypnosis for weight loss. The hypnosis session is designed to help the student override their desire to eat certain foods. The hypnotist tells the student, that he/she does not like junk food. Those sweet foods leave a sour taste in the student's mouth. Also sweets make the student sick. This student already has A PRE-THOUGHT in his/her belief system. Such as I like junk food. Junk food makes me fat. He/She also may have a feeling of low self-esteem. This all gets into his/her PRE-THOUGHT (SUBCONSCIOUS). Thoughts MAY come out like this: I like junk food. Junk food makes me fat. Every time I eat junk food it makes me sick. THE KEY IS WORK ON SELF-IMAGE FIRST! THE KEY TO A BETTER SELF-IMAGE IS NON-JUDGMENT. FORGIVENESS IS THE FIRST STEP TO NON-JUDGMENT. THE BODY IS THE PRODUCT OF VOICED AFFIRMATION (I AM).

It is important to forgive yourself, for any "excess weight" you may perceive to have. YOU MAY STOP SAYING THE VOICED AFFIRMATION: I AM FAT! No matter what I eat I cannot lose weight! These statements create your body image. Replace these statements with the truth. My body has served me based on my beliefs and affirmations. I release the fat because I no longer need it. I will choose a method of weight loss, which is based on my belief system. Through voiced affirmations I AM slim and healthy!

There are people who can eat anything they want and never gain weight. When they are told not to eat so much they will inform you that they can eat what ever they want and never gain weight. These people are an example of their body being a voiced affirmation I AM, and so is yours. The information in your belief system and voiced affirmation attract energy and create a magnetic field around you what brings into your life what your belief system dictates.

CHAPTER TWENTY TWO

THE THREE-FOLD PHASE OF MANIFESTATION

MIND = THOUGHT

BODY = VOICED AFFIRMATION

SOUL = BELIEF (AGREEMENT)

STEP 1. THOUGHT—Alone it is without form, MANIFESTATION.

STEP 2. SPOKEN WORD—Belief through the spoken word.

STEP 3. FAITH—The belief it will happen (NO DOUBT)!

THOUGHT + SPOKEN WORD + BELIEF = MANIFESTATION
THOUGHTS ARE THINGS IN THE PROCESS OF BEING CREATED.

FOCUS YOUR THOUGHTS WITH DIRECTION
1. EONS (PRE-THOUGHT)
2. IMAGINATION, which attracts eons and forms them into ions, electrons, and protons. Imagination has the ability

to create. The thought attracts them creating protons and electrons and bring them together in agreement, the (ATOM). When we have pure thought, without judgment, time stops. No time element because, so I say and so it is. FOCUS thoughts with direction.

3. RESULT no time element. As I say it is, (so it is)!

NOTE: CONFLICTING THOUGHTS BOUNCING AROUND CREATE INTERESTING RESULTS.

THE AGREEMENT

As I have come into UNIVERSAL CONSCIOUSNESS, my mind becomes less full and my thoughts are put to rest. I need not analyze or contemplate, because at a glance I know and understand all.

UNIVERSAL CONSCIOUSNESS, simply put is SELF-ACCEPTANCE and SELF-LOVE.

ACCEPTANCE is the key to unlock the door to set you eternally free!

CHAPTER TWENTY-THREE

UNCONDITIONAL LOVE

STEP 1. Love yourself.

STEP 2. Love yourself.

STEP 3. Love yourself.

STEP 4. Perceive no separation. See that everyone is an extension of you.

STEP 5. Love yourself.

STUDENT: How do I make contact with my angel guides?

ANGEL: Through prayer and meditation. Through these methods you will reunite yourself with your counterparts.

STUDENT: How many angel guides does a person have?

ANGEL: As many as needed for the experience of non-separation.

STUDENT: How do I get to experience unconditional love?

ANGEL: Love yourself first! Unconditional love is the key
            to all happiness and abundance.

                    LOVE = SELF-ACCEPTANCE
                    KARMA = SELF-CONDEMNATION
                    FREE WILL = YOUR CHOICE

IF I TRULY LOVE MYSELF, I LOVE YOU BECAUSE YOU
ARE SIMPLY AN EXTENSION OF MYSELF.

UNCONDITIONAL LOVE gives freely because there is no
separation; therefore if I give to you I truly give to myself. A
word of caution, never give anything that you wish to keep for
yourself. You must always give freely. It would be better to keep
something than to give it half hearted. To your own self be true.
Half hearted giving causes karma. Follow the steps to achieve
unconditional love. Love yourself first and give freely to yourself
first. Than you will have a feeling of abundance and will be able
to give freely to others.

STUDENT: When I let go of opinion (JUDGMENT), what
            will be left to speak of?
ANGEL: TRUTH (ONENESS)
STUDENT: How do I let go of JUDGMENT?
ANGEL: Realize that we all are one. That when you speak
            to anyone you truly speak to To yourself. As you
            judge others you truly judge yourself.

STUDENT: I believe this to be the truth, yet I find it hard to do.

ANGEL: Treat others, as you want to be treated yourself. Remember that as you give you truly Receive.

LOVE IS THE KEY

If 100 people love me and I do not love myself. I would feel unloved and empty. The only way to ever feel loved is to give love daily to (yourself), which means everyone.

We are all one. The amount of love that flows from you will come back three fold.

Three fold means: MIND, BODY AND SOUL in continuous flow. SIMPLY PUT: THE ONLY WAY TO FEEL LOVE IS TO LOVE.

STUDENT: I want to love myself, yet I don't always like myself because of my actions.

ANGEL: LET GO OF THE JUDGMENT.

LET GO OF THE GUILT.

LET GO OF THE ANGER.

LET GO OF THE HATE.

LET GO OF THE JEALOUSY.

LET GO OF THE LONELINESS.

LET GO OF THE SEPARATION.

SIMPLY PUT: LET GO AND ACKNOWLEDGE THE GOD IN YOURSELF AND IN EVERYONE ELSE.

STUDENT: I want to acknowledge GOD in others and myself yet; it seems so difficult at times, where do I start?

ANGEL: Acceptance is the key. The way to let go of quilt, is to accept your actions WITHOUT JUDGMENT of them and in order to do that you must ACCEPT all actions of others, Without judgment. Remember we are all one. Since we are co-creators with the Father, we chose these experiences and so did they in order to grow and learn. It was Always your choice and since we are one it was always their choice also.

THE AGREEMENT WAS MADE ON ANOTHER LEVEL OF CONSCIOUSNESS. EVEN WHEN THE EXPERIENCE SEEMS BAD (JUDGMENT), IF ONE LOOKS WITH THE SINGLE EYE (WITHOUT JUDGMENT) WE WILL SEE THAT THESE PEOPLE WERE OUR GREATEST TEACHERS.

STUDENT: What is betrayal?

ANGEL: Betrayal comes when someone does not do what we want and expect them to do. It is When we judge what is appropriate behavior.

STUDENT: Can anyone hurt someone without his or her permission?

ANGEL: Remember free will. Betrayal does not exist. It is simply a word given to mask our True feelings.

Self-Betrayal is simply GIVING OUR POWER TO SOMEONE ELSE FOR OUR HAPPINESS OR OUR UNHAPPINESS. BETRAYAL DOES NOT EXIST BECAUSE NO ONE HAS THE POWER TO CONTROL YOUR THOUGHTS AND FEELING EXCEPT YOU. The way you feel and react is always Your choice. JESUS said, "Be in the world but not of it". The statement means: Do Not react the way others may desire you to react. Remember to your own self be true.

STUDENT: How do I let go of feeling of betrayal?

ANGEL: Acknowledge no one has the power to make us feel anything. Remember we Have "FREE WILL". The choice is ours. Realize that betrayal does not exist Let go of expectations of yourself and others. Never do anything for someone Else unless you really want to. Give only when you can give freely without expecting Give only when you can give freely without expecting something in return. Realize That when you give you receive NOT THAT "you owe me".

HAVING COME TO THE REALIZATION THAT EVER-ONE IS A MIRROR BECAUSE WE ARE ONE. THEREFORE AS I GIVE TO YOU, I TRULY GIVE TO MYSELF.

CHAPTER TWENTY-FOUR

STEPS TO REMOVE ANGER

MENTAL (ACKNOWLEDGEMENT)
PHYSICAL (RELEASE ADRENALINE)
SPIRITUAL (UNCONDITIONAL LOVE)

STEP 1.   MENTAL—Acknowledge that you are angry. Do not judge your feeling saying to Yourself: I cannot feel like this because I am spiritual. Realizing that to be spiritual one must live in the moment of now. If you have these feelings acknowledge them because this is the first step in realizing them. Allow yourself to feel anger.

STEP 2.   PHYSICAL—Release anger (ADRENALINE). When we feel anger our adrenaline Rises. In order to calm ourselves, we must release the physical symptoms. To release the adrenaline one must do physical activity. There are various methods such as: physical exercises, clean your house, hit a punching bag, hit the couch with a pillow, walk, run or take deep breaths to release the adrenaline.

STEP 3. SPIRITUAL—Realize that no one has control over your emotions but you. If someone pushes your buttons it is your CHOICE to get angry. You now realize, that no one can control or hurt you, unless you decide that they can hurt you. It is your choice and in essence you really hurt yourself. Many times we feel that people hurt us when they do not live up to our expectations. They do not treat us in a way we feel we deserve to be treated. Therefore it is not their actions or lack of actions that hurt us. It is truly our unfulfilled expectations that disappoint or anger us.

WE NOW CAN REMEMBER ABOUT UNCONDITIONAL LOVE, WHICH IS BOTH SELF-ACCEPTANCE AND ACCEPTANCE OF OTHERS. ACCEPTANCE OF OTHER AS THEY ARE AND NOT AS WE THINK THEY SHOULD BE.

CHAPTER TWENTY-FIVE

MOTIVES

(JUSTIFICATION + DENIAL = KARMA)

Karma is merely the fact of cause and effect. It is the process of one action resulting in a chain Reaction of choices. Your life is simply a series of choices. The basics for your choices are your thoughts, which includes your beliefs, desires and fears. Our actions are a result of our belief system. These beliefs or values are then manifested in the physical by our own choices. Our life is based on our own belief system in which we base our actions which in turn creates our life, as we know it. If we change our thoughts we will truly change our life. Avoidance of what my be termed as negative karma is a simple process check your motives and you will understand the possible results.

CHAPTER TWENTY-SIX

HOW TO CHECK YOUR MOTIVES

STEP 1. HAVE THE WILLINGNESS TO BE HONEST WITH YOURSELF.

STEP 2. CHECK YOUR MOTIVES.

For every action there is a chain reaction: Therefore to understand your motives is to understand the possibilities of a chain reaction.

STEP 3. LOOK PAST THE OBVIOUS REASON.

Many choices are deep seated in our own belief system, which includes our desires, needs and fears. To understand why we wish to do these actions is to understand the result. We are co-creators with GOD; therefore we know what we are creating. Our subconscious knows that which we wish to experience based on our own personal reality.

STEP 4.   ASK FOR HELP.

Ask for help from your GOD source. We need not examine our motives alone. Our angel guides both of the physical and non-physical are of service to us.

STEP 5.   HAVE FAITH.

Know that as you ask the truth shall be given.

STEP 6.   MAKE CHOICES IN THE LIGHT OF TRUTH.

Having received the information of our true motives in the light of truth we may now understand the outcome of our choices. We may chose to receive the lesson or we may now choose to change some of our old patterns and beliefs. The choice is ultimately yours.

NO CHOICE IS NEGATIVE OR BAD. THE LESSON MAY BE LEARNED BY INTERNAL UNDERSTANDING OR IN THE PHYSICAL. THE CHOICE IS ULTIMATELY YOURS.

CHAPTER TWENTY-SEVEN

UNIVERSAL LAWS FOR LIVING

STEP 1. Ask GOD to have communion with you through prayer and meditation.

STEP 2. Develop faith: Believe that as you ask for help it will be given.

STEP 3. Write down all experiences in this lifetime and take an honest look at yourself.

STEP 4. Develop trust: Confess all experiences to at least one other person. All secrets must Cease to exist!

STEP 5. Develop self-acceptance and acceptance of others.

LET GO OF EXPECTATIONS = LETTING GO OF PAIN.

LET GO OF DISAPPOINTMENT = LET GO OF EXPECTATIONS.

LET GO OF ANGER = LET GO OF EXPECTATIONS.

LET GO OF FEAR = LET GO OF JUDGMENT/SEPARATION.

THE KEY FOR SELF-ACCEPTANCE AND ACCEPTANCE OF OTHERS IS LETTING GO OF EXPECTATIONS, WHICH IN TURN

WILL LEAD TO NON-JUDGMENT AND NON/SEPARATION; WHICH LEADS TO UNCONDITIONAL LOVE, WHICH IS TRUTH.

STEP 6.   Develop self-forgiveness and forgiveness' of others.

THE KEY IS ACCEPTANCE THAT PEOPLE HAVE NOT LIVED UP TO OUR EXPECTATIONS, AND ACCEPTANCE THAT WE HAVE NOT ALWAYS LIVED UP TO OUR OWN EXPECTATIONS OF OURSELVES. ACCEPTANCE THAT WE CANNOT CONTROL OTHERS AND ACCEPTANCE THAT OTHERS CANNOT CONTROL US WITH OUT OUR CONSENT.

STEP 7.   Now I am a teacher of truth. I practice the UNIVERSAL LAWS FOR LIVING DAILY. I now apply the UNIVERSAL LAWS FOR LIVING DAILY with each new experience.

GO AND SPREAD THE NEWS GOD IS ALIVE AND WITH YOU ALWAYS. YOU ARE A LIGHT OF THE WORLD. GOD BLESSES!